To Zoe and Sigurd
— F.T.

First American Edition 2020
Kane Miller, A Division of EDC Publishing
P.O. Box 470663, Tulsa, OK 74147-0663
www.kanemiller.com
Text by Harriet Evans
Text copyright © Caterpillar Books Ltd 2020
Illustrations copyright © Fotini Tikkou 2020
Library of Congress Control Number: 2019952412
ISBN: 978-1-68464-057-7
Printed in China
CPB/1400/1541/0720
10 9 8 7 6 5 4 3 2

FAMILY HEROES

Keeping Us Healthy

Illustrated by Fotini Tikkou

Kane Miller
A DIVISION OF EDC PUBLISHING

My parents are amazing,

healing people every day.

They handle any problem,

whatever comes their way.

My daddy is a nurse,

he's as caring as can be.

He cheers up all his patients, and then comes home to me.

My mommy is a doctor,
she helps people when they're ill.
Her knowledge is unrivaled,
she's commended for her skill.

My daddy drives an ambulance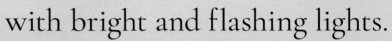

with bright and flashing lights.

He's dedicated to his job,

he works both days and nights.

My mommy captures X-rays on a great big white machine.

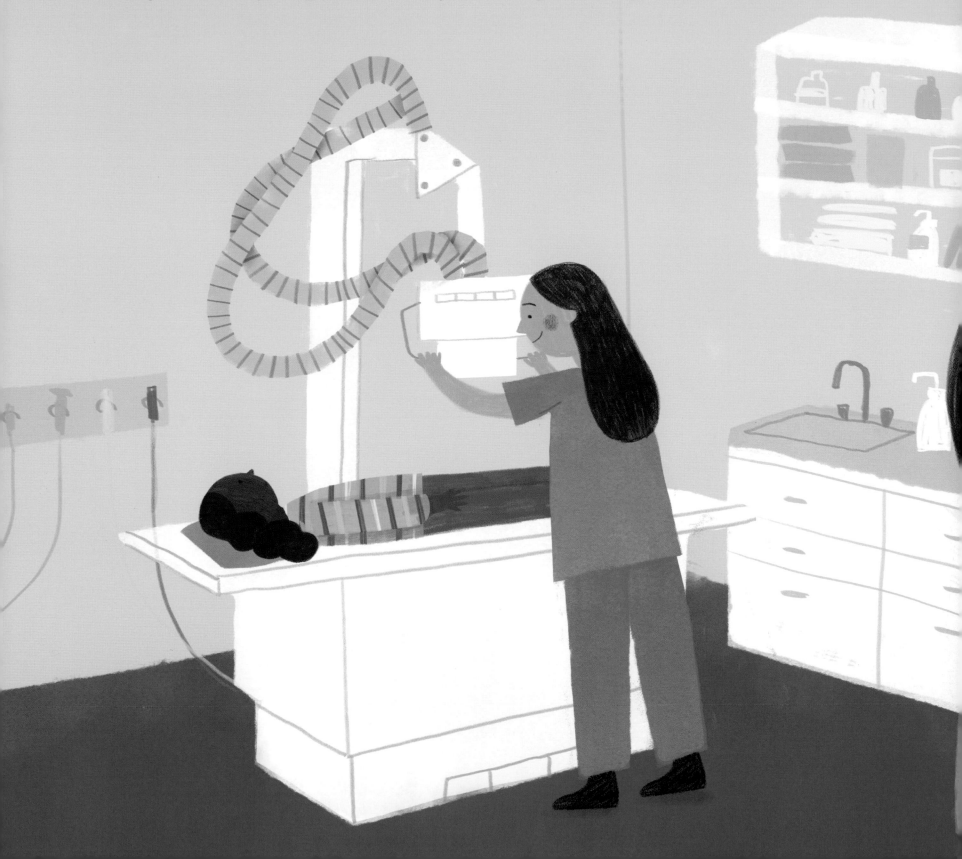

She works out why we're hurting

from the pictures on her screen.

My daddy is a pharmacist, dispensing medication.

He's happiest when giving help,

and says that's his vocation.

My mommy is a dentist.
She'll make your teeth so strong.

She'll answer all your questions,
and help to fix what's wrong.

My daddy is an eye doctor,

he tends to people's vision.

And when he's fixing eyesight,

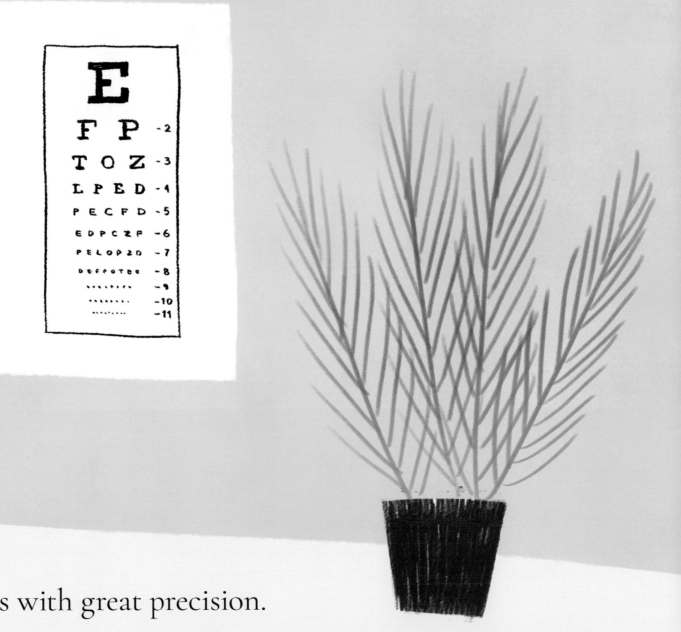

he works with great precision.

My mommy aids recovery,

she helps patients learn to walk.

She's really good at listening, if you ever need to talk.

My daddy works with animals.
He's a kind, inspiring vet.

And every single evening,
he helps me feed my pet.

My mommy flies above the clouds

and saves people from up high.

She's coming to the rescue,

a real hero in the sky.

My parents are amazing,

healing people every day.

They handle any problem,

whatever comes their way.

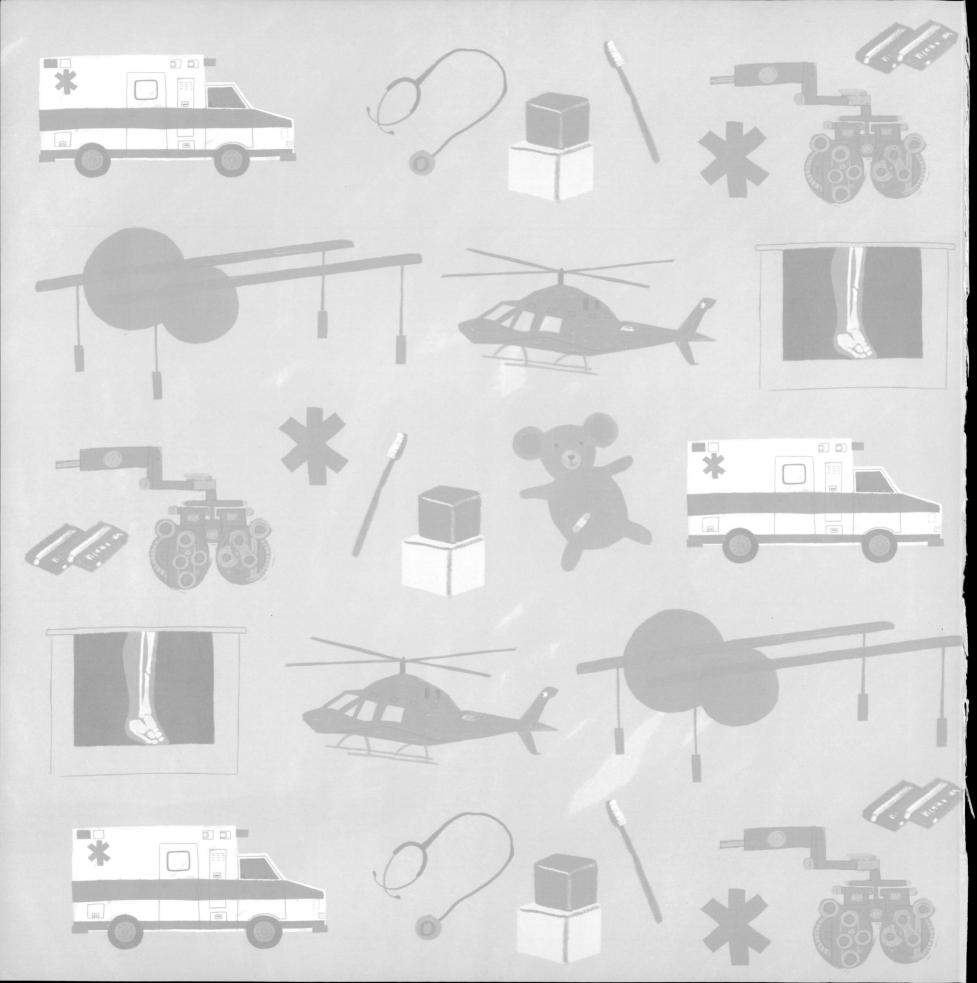